Searching Issues
Manual

Published 1996
Reprint 1 September 1997
Revised edition June 1998
Reprinted January 1999
Reprinted August 1999

Published by HTB Publications,
Holy Trinity Brompton, Brompton Road,
London SW7 1JA

Printed in the UK by TPS Print, 6 Warren Lane, London, SE18 6BW
Telephone: 0208 317 2997

CONTENTS

1
WHY DOES GOD ALLOW SUFFERING?

	Notes

INTRODUCTION

Most frequently raised objection

Greatest single challenge to the Christian faith in every generation

- Global suffering
- Community suffering
- Individual suffering

Seeming contradiction between suffering and an all-loving, all-powerful God

I. HUMAN FREEDOM

Suffering not part of creation (Genesis 1-2, Revelation 21)

Sin of Adam and Eve led to beginning of suffering

All suffering is a result of sin, directly or indirectly

Reasons for and consequences of free will

a) Our own sin

Suffering can be:

- ◆ inevitable consequence

eg drug abuse, reckless driving

♦ God actively judging (2 Kings 5:27; Acts 5:1-11)

No automatic link between sin and suffering (Job 42:7-8)

Jesus expressly repudiates automatic link

(Luke 13:1-5; John 9:1-3)

Extra distinction: (1 Peter 2:19, 20)

Danger of making judgements re. others' suffering

b) Sin of others

♦ Global eg war, starvation

♦ Community eg Dunblane (1996), Aberfan (1966)

♦ Individual eg murder, adultery, theft, abuse, unloving parents

c) Sin of Adam

Disorder in creation - fallen world (Genesis 3:18; Romans 8:20)

Natural disasters

Freedom explains the origin of suffering but does not answer the question "Why me?"

II. GOD WORKS THROUGH SUFFERING

He uses it for good

- ◆ Draws us to Christ
- ◆ Brings us to Christian maturity (Hebrews 5:8)
  - Disciplining towards holiness (Hebrews 12:10, 11)
  - Refining towards purity (1 Peter 1:7)
  - Pruning towards fruitfulness (John 15:2)
- ◆ Brings about his purposes (Romans 8:28; Genesis 50:20)
- ◆ Some suffering we cannot comprehend

III. GOD MORE THAN COMPENSATES FOR OUR SUFFERING

For some in this life eg Joseph, Job

For all Christians, there is the hope of heaven

(Romans 8:18;
2 Corinthians 4:17)

Maintaining an eternal perspective - a new heaven and a new earth (Revelation 21:1)

Notes

Notes

CONCLUSION

How do we respond?

- ◆ Three questions to ask God:

  - Is this suffering a result of my own sin? (If so, ask for God's forgiveness and cleansing)

  - What are you saying to me through this?

  - What do you want me to do?

- ◆ Hold on to our hope (Hebrews 12:2)

- ◆ When we see others suffering, we are called to show compassion and take action

- ◆ Resist suffering as alien intrusion in God's world

- ◆ Come back to the cross (God suffering for us and with us) of Christ and his resurrection (the promise of eternity)

2
WHAT ABOUT OTHER RELIGIONS?

INTRODUCTION

Statistics: Encyclopedia
Britannica

- 1700 million
  Christians = 32.9% of
  world population
- 880 million Muslims
- 663 million Hindus
- 311 million Buddhists

Many other smaller groupings

Atheists = 4.5% of world
population

I. IS JESUS THE ONLY WAY TO GOD?

The New Testament answer:
'yes'

(John 14:6)

(1 Timothy 2:5)

(Acts 4:12)

(Hebrews 2:3)

Notes

Notes

What makes Jesus unique?

- ◆ His qualification (Acts 3:14)

- ◆ His achievement (Acts 4:12)

- ◆ His resurrection (Acts 4:10)

II. WHAT DO WE SAY ABOUT OTHER RELIGIONS?

Jesus: "I am the truth"

Jesus is the standard by which all truth claims are to be tested. But we would expect to find truth in other religions for at least three reasons:

- ◆ God has partially revealed himself in creation (Psalm 19:1, Romans 1:20)

- ◆ Human beings are made in the image of God. We have been given a conscience with which to distinguish right and wrong (Romans 2:14-15)

- ◆ In every human heart there is a hunger for God (Ecclesiastes 3:11)

III. WHAT ABOUT THOSE WHO HAVE NEVER HEARD ABOUT JESUS?

- Hypothetical question - can only be asked by someone who *has* heard about Jesus

- We can be sure God will be just (Genesis 18:25)

- No one will be saved by their religion (Ephesians 2:8)

- It is possible to be saved by grace through faith even if someone has never heard of Jesus (Romans 4:3; Romans 4:6, Luke 18:9-14)

- There are biblical grounds for great optimism (Genesis 22:17; Romans 5:2)

IV. WHY SHOULD WE BOTHER TO TELL OTHERS ABOUT JESUS?

- The glory of Jesus Christ is at stake

- Jesus commanded us to go into all the world and tell the good news

- Without knowing about Jesus no one can have assurance of forgiveness and the abundant life he offers

Notes

Notes

CONCLUSION

Our response must be to tell people the good news about Jesus

- Be humble
- Be sensitive
- Be positive
- Be respectful
- Be courageous

3

Is there Anything Wrong with Sex Before Marriage?

Introduction

Obsession of the modern era

Concurrent breakdown in family life

Repressive attitude of former times

What is the Biblical understanding?

I. God, in his love, has given us a good plan

◆ The Bible affirms our sexuality (Genesis 1:27)

- The body is good (Psalm 139:14)

- The sexual urge is God-given (Genesis 2:25)

◆ The Bible celebrates sexual intimacy (Genesis 4:1)

Song of Songs: delight, tenderness,

contentment and satisfaction

- ◆ Sex in its right context is good and beautiful (Ephesians 5)

- ◆ The biblical context for sexual intercourse is the life-long commitment in marriage between one man and one woman

  Creation account (Genesis 2:24)

  (Matthew 19:5-6)

  - Leaving

  - Uniting

  - 'One flesh' sexual union

- ◆ Partnership and procreation are linked (Genesis 1:28)

II. GOD, IN HIS LOVE, WARNS AGAINST HUMAN DISTORTIONS

- ◆ Sin affects every area of human lives, including sexuality (Romans 3:23)

  None of us is in a position to pass judgement (John 8:7)

  Nevertheless sin does matter (John 8:11)

- ◆ Any sex outside marriage is a distortion of God's good gift and falls short of his ideal

    This includes adultery and sex before marriage

    (1 Corinthians 6:16, 18; Mark 7:21; 1 Thessalonians 4:3-8)

- ◆ When God's pattern is broken people get hurt

    - We risk hurting ourselves

    - We risk hurting others

    - We risk hurting society

    - We hurt God

God will judge all sin (1 Thessalonians 4:6)

III. GOD, IN HIS LOVE, SENT JESUS TO RESTORE US

Jesus did not come to condemn the world but to save it, giving us the power to resist temptation, and bring forgiveness and healing (God can enable individuals to control their sexual urges)

a) How to resist

- ◆ Jesus began with the heart, the eyes and the thoughts (Matthew 5:28)

Notes

- We need to help one another by not putting temptation in the way
- Is masturbation a way out?

  Not physically harmful and it is nowhere specifically condemned in the Bible

  Three concerns:

  - Tendency to become obsessive

  - Depersonalises sex

  - Often associated with lustful thoughts

b) Forgiveness

All of us have failed in this area to greater or lesser extent

Way to receive forgiveness is through repentance (Psalm 51)

CONCLUSION

The heart of our sexuality is not the biological dimension but the personal one

Christians must worship God himself, not his gifts

- If we treat pleasure as a god, in the long-run we find emptiness, disappointment and addiction

- If we seek God, we find complete fulfilment

4

How does the New Age Movement Relate to Christianity?

Introduction

Cultural shift from "Enlightenment" to "Post-modernity"

One strand is New Age movement

Emphasises experience and values spirituality

Highlights emptiness and shortcomings of rationalism and materialism

I. What is the New Age movement?

Umbrella term that covers various diverse movements, beliefs and lifestyles. Impossible to define - no leader, no organisation, no headquarters

Mixture of Eastern mysticism and occult practices which have been given a Western materialistic flavour

May include self-improvement programmes, holistic health, concern for world peace, ecology and spiritual enlightenment

NOTE:

- ◆ Many New Age teachings are derived from Eastern mysticism, TM, reincarnation, karma, Zen, yoga and levitation

- ◆ Influence of nature religions from around the world, including Druidism and Wicca witchcraft

- ◆ A number of practices in the movement overtly occult and condemned in the Bible eg astrology (horoscopes), fortune-telling, clairvoyance, consulting the dead, spiritism, mediums, channelling, spirit guides and tarot cards

    (Deuteronomy 18:10)

    (Leviticus 19:26, 31)

    (Galatians 5:20)

    (Revelation 9:20-21)

    Influence of the movement everywhere: arts and music, bookshops, interna tional capitalism, films, videos and computer games, even church

II. WHAT ARE THE BELIEFS OF THE NEW AGE MOVEMENT?

John Stott's summary

◆ All is God - 'pantheism'

No distinction between the Creator and what he has created

A self-centred movement: God within us.

Focus on self - opposite of Christianity

◆ All is one - 'monism'

Rejection of moral absolutes

'Sin' is not a popular word

Guidance comes from 'within' - "if it feels good, do it."

Everyone is eventually making progress onwards and upwards towards spiritual enlightenment and perfection. No judgement - contrary to Christianity

(Genesis 3:4; Hebrews 9:27)

Notes

Notes

◆ All is well - optimism

   Evolutionary progress
   towards Utopia

III. WHAT IS WRONG WITH THE NEW AGE MOVEMENT?

Some things linked to the
New Age movement are
themselves good, such as:

- The challenge to
  prevailing
  materialism and
  rationalism

- The emphasis on the
  importance of
  experience and the
  high value put on
  spirituality

- The focus on
  compassion, love and
  unity

- The search for
  spiritual reality

But it falls way short of the
glorious truths of Christianity:

a) It does not get near the
truth about God the Father

◆ God thought of as
  impersonal, abstract
  force

◆ Men and women were
  made to live in a
  personal relationship of

love and worship of God

*"You have made us
yourself, and our heart is
restless until   it rests in
you"*
                St.Augustine

b) It does not get near the
truth about God the Son

♦ Jesus is seen merely as
  one of the 'ascended
  masters', along with
  Buddha, Krishna and
  others

♦ Jesus Christ is in fact
  *"the way, and the truth
  and the life"* (John 14:6)

♦ New Age discounts the
  cross and resurrection -
  the only true means of
  salvation

c) It does not get near the
truth about God the Holy
Spirit

♦ The search for spiritual
  power, spiritual
  experience and
  transformed lives is
  fruitless without the
  Holy Spirit

♦ The Holy Spirit
  transforms Christians
  into the likeness of Jesus
  Christ and enables them
  to have an inpact on
  society (2 Corinthians
  3:18 Galatians 5:22-23)

Notes

Notes

CONCLUSION

What response should we make?

a) Need for a double repentance

- ◆ If we've been involved in New Age practices we need to ask God's forgivenss, turn to Jesus Christ and ask the Holy Spirit to come and live in our lives

- ◆ Those of us involved in the church need to repent of our rigidity, rationalism and failure to make the church relevant to the culture in which we live

b) We need to soak ourselves in the truth (Colossians 2:8; 2 Timothy 4:3-5)

c) We need to bring the good news of Jesus to those who are involved in the New Age, demonstrating by our lives (both individually and as the church) the supernatural power of God: Father, Son and Holy Spirit

5
WHAT IS THE CHRISTIAN ATTITUDE TO HOMOSEXUALITY?

INTRODUCTION

The Bible is the story of God's love for all humanity. God loves all people, irrespective of race, colour, background or sexual orientation. As we approach this subject, I am conscious of the agony that exists for many people in this area. Jesus came not to condemn us, but to save (John 3:17). In the same way, the Christian community needs to show sensitivity and understanding towards those for whom their homosexual orientation is a daily struggle, and to affirm them as human beings loved by God

The gay liberation movement 'urge the view that homosexuality is a natural variant of human sexuality - as natural as red hair or left-handedness - to be affirmed and rejoiced in, and that its expression in fully loving physical sexual embrace is well within the purpose and will of God'

I. Is homosexual practice an option for a Christian?

Biblical view of sexual intercourse is positive and liberating

Context is lifelong commitment (in marriage) between one man and one woman (Genesis 2: 24)

Our bodies were not designed for homosexual intercourse

The view of marriage and sex, which Jesus quoted and endorsed, rules out all sex outside marriage, whether heterosexual or homosexual

All references to homosexual practice in the Bible are negative:

(Leviticus 18:22; 20:13)

(Judges 19:23)

(1 Corinthians 6:9-10; 1 Timothy 1:9)

(1 Corinthians 6:11)

(Romans 1:24-27) Nowhere does the Bible condemn homosexual orientation, homosexual feelings or homosexual temptation

Temptation is not sin
(Hebrews 4:15)

The Bible does not condemn
homosexual preference, but
homosexual practice

II. IS AIDS THE JUDGEMENT OF GOD ON HOMOSEXUAL PRACTICE?

We can look at biblical
principles and seek to apply
them to a modern disease

Two different types of
judgement:

a) *"effectus"* - inevitable result
of sin

b) *"affectus"* - God's personal
reaction against sin.

Is AIDS "effectus" or
"affectus"?

- ◆ One day God will judge
the world - he will be
perfectly fair and just
- ◆ God sometimes
intervenes as a judge in
this life (Genesis 19;
Acts 5)
- ◆ Supernatural acts of
intervening judgement
are rare, but his
judgement in the sense of

the inevitable results of sin is ongoing

AIDS cannot be seen as a one-off judgement of God "affectus" on homosexuality since 90% of the new infections world-wide are heterosexual

Some are infected through blood transfusions and others inherit from their parents

However, AIDS can be seen as a consequence of breaking God's rules relating to sexual morality "effectus"

God's rules were given to protect people from getting hurt

When his laws are broken, it is often not only the law breaker who is hurt, but innocent people too

We were not designed for homosexual or promiscuous activity

Best way to stop spread of AIDS - return to biblical standards

AIDS only a symptom of real crisis in society - separation from God

III. *CAN SEXUAL ORIENTATION BE CHANGED?*

All our hopes are based on the cross of Christ

- ◆ Forgiveness for the past
- ◆ Power for the present

(1 Corinthians 6:9-11;
1 Corinthians 10:13)

Is it possible to change?

- ◆ No conclusive scientific evidence that genetic or hormonal factors are causative in homosexual behaviour. Often acquired or learned

- ◆ Almost certainly not that person's fault

- ◆ Homosexuality is not part of the original created order, but an indirect result of sin entering the world. Therefore we should seek restoration and healing. For some, healing may take place now in this life; for others, later (Romans 8:23)

- ◆ Examples of forgivenss, healing and new sexual wholeness in Christ

IV. *WHAT SHOULD OUR ATTITUDE BE TO THOSE INVOLVED IN A HOMOSEXUAL LIFESTYLE?*

We are all fallen: none of us is in a position to throw stones at others (John 8:7)

Our calling is to follow Christ's example, which is to love and accept people unconditionally

At the same time, we must recognise sin as sin, rather than condoning it (John 8:11): this is part of love

- ◆ Speak out where appropriate against the PRACTICE of homosexuality

- ◆ Love *all* people and welcome them with open arms into the church

- ◆ Promote a safe environment where the homesexually orientated can find somebody with whom they can talk and pray

- ◆ The church should be at the forefront of bringing hope and healing to those with AIDS

CONCLUSION

Love is the key from first to last

- ◆ In his love, God gave us sex
- ◆ In his love, he also gave us boundaries
- ◆ In his love, he sent Jesus to bring us forgiveness and the power to resist temptation and bring us healing

We are called to be like him and to go out and love as he loved us

Notes

Notes

6

*I*S THERE A CONFLICT BETWEEN SCIENCE AND CHRISTIANITY?

*I*NTRODUCTION

Popular belief is that science and Christianity are in direct conflict

Two reasons:

a) Times in history when the church has opposed the results of scientific study eg Galileo and the Roman Catholic Church

b) Popular thinking that modern scientific study explains everything that was once explained by belief in God

*I. S*CIENCE AND *C*HRISTIAN *FAITH ARE NOT INCOMPATIBLE*

The Christian worldview provided the right

environment for modern science to emerge

◆ The Christian faith is monotheistic

Belief in one God led people to expect a uniformity in nature, with the underlying laws of nature remaining the same in space and time

◆ The Christian doctrine of creation by a rational God of order led scientists to expect a world which was both ordered and intelligible

◆ The Christian belief in a transcendent God, separate from nature, meant that experimentation was justified

For much of history Christianity and scientific study have been allies not opponents

- Copernicus (1473-1543)

- Galileo (1564-1642)

- Kepler (1571-1630)

- Newton (1642-1727)

- Faraday (1791-1867)

Robert Boyle, Joseph Lister, Louis Pasteur, Gregor Mendel,

Lord Kelvin, James Maxwell, James Simpson

II. *SCIENCE AND SCRIPTURE DO NOT CONTRADICT EACH OTHER*

Alleged conflicts between science and theology:

- Spinoza (1632-1677): nothing can 'contravene nature's universal laws'

- Hume: a miracle is 'a violation of the laws of nature' and consequently impossible (circular argument: supernatural ruled out from start)

a) Miracles

A knowledge of laws of nature essential in order to recognise miracles ie - not natural for someone to rise from the dead

The real issue is 'Is there a God?' If there is, then miracles become a real possibility

"I'm not suggesting that miracles are an adequate basis for theism. But, once we have come on other grounds to believe in God... it becomes logical to affirm, and

illogical to deny, the possibility of the miraculous. For 'natural laws' describe God's activity; they do not control it."

John Stott

b) Evolution

Much of the theory of evolution is still only a theory

◆ Micro-evolution: development within a species - could not conceivably be said to conflict with the Bible

◆ Macro-evolution: evolution from one species to another (eg apes to humans). Still unproven and remains a theory which is not accepted by all scientists

There are many different interpretations of Genesis held by sincere Christians

◆ Literal six-day creation

◆ Others point out that the Hebrew word 'day' has many different meanings, even within Scripture - can mean a long period of time

◆ Others see Genesis 1 not necessarily connected with chronological events in history. It is a pre-scientific and non-scientific account of creation, dealing with matters outside the scope of science

Main point of Genesis 1 is not to answer the questions 'How?' and 'When?' (scientific), but the questions 'Why?' and 'Who?' (theological questions)

The Bible offers a personal explanation rather than a scientific one

III. SCIENCE AND SCRIPTURE COMPLEMENT EACH OTHER

Science is the study of God's general self-revelation in creation

Biblical theology is the study of God's 'special' revelation in Jesus

(Psalm 19:1-4a; Romans 1:20; Acts 14:17; 17:22-28)

"Science without religion is lame"   Einstein

God has made a world where there is much to suggest his presence:

◆ Causation argument

◆ Evidence of design

General revelation suggests

the tremendous power, intelligence and imagination of a personal creator

- ◆ We cannot find the God of the Bible through science alone. Only by God's special revelation can we find *"the God and Father of our Lord Jesus Christ"*

- ◆ Science cannot speak to the deepest needs of men and women (including scientists!)

  - It cannot deal with the problems of loneliness or hearts broken by grief

  - No answer to moral dilemmas

  - No remedy for the problem of unforgiven sin and guilt

Only in the cross of Christ do we find the answer to these problems

CONCLUSION

We need science and scientists. Our civilisation owes a great deal to their work. But, more importantly, we need Christianity and Jesus Christ

7

Is the Trinity Unbiblical, Unbelievable and Irrelevant?

Introduction

Derived from the Latin word 'trinitas', which means 'threeness'

tri-personality of God

1. Is it biblical?

The word 'Trinity' does not appear in the Bible

First used in its Greek form by Theophilus, Bishop of Antioch in c. AD180

"Let us not be misled by the foolish argument that because the term 'Trinity' does not occur in the scriptures, the doctrine of the Trinity is therefore unscriptual."
F.F.Bruce

Christianity arose out of Judaism - monotheistic faith. New Testament affirms only one God

(John 5:44; Romans 3:30; 1 Timothy 1:17; James 2:19)

Early Christians faced two historical events which revolutionised their understanding of God

- ◆ The revelatory events of the life, death and resurrection of Jesus Christ

- ◆The experience of the Holy Spirit at Pentecost

Came to believe in the deity of the Father, the deity of the Son and the deity of the Holy Spirit: yet they still believed there was only one God (see eg John's gospel)

Concept of Trinity permeates pages of New Testament

Some suggest hint in Old Testament eg (Genesis 1:1-3a)

New Testament: several trinitarian formulae:

- ◆ Baptism into the name (singular) of the Father and the Son and the Holy Spirit (Matthew 28:19)

- ◆ The Grace (2 Corinthians 13:14)

While these two texts do not expressly state the doctrine of the Trinity, they point strongly towards it

◆ Paul sees virtually every aspect of the Christian faith and Christian life in trinitarian terms

Gifts of the Spirit
(1 Corinthians 12:4-6)

- Prayer
(Ephesians 2:18)

- Fullness of the Spirit
(Ephesians 3:14-19)

- Unity
(Ephesians 4: 3-6)

- Ethical instruction
(Ephesians 4)

- Worship
(Ephesians 5:18-20)

- Salvation
(2 Thessalonians 2:13,14)

Also Peter:

- Election
(1 Peter 1:1-2)

Yet, no formal credal statement about the Trinity

Early church forced into defining a coherent and

systematic doctrine against the heretical views which were being expounded:

a) Polytheism

b) One person with three names (Sabellius reduced the Trinity to a unity with three modes of expression)

- ◆ Council of Constantinople in AD 381, building on the Council of Nicaea in AD 325, spoke of one God and three persons
- ◆ Athanasian creed:

> *"We worship one God in Trinity, and Trinity in Unity, neither confounding the Persons nor dividing the Divine Being. For there is one Person of the Father, another of the Son, and another the Holy Spirit: but the Godhead of the Father, the Son and the Holy Spirit is all one."*

II. IS IT BELIEVABLE?

Not easy to understand

Dealing with the nature of God himself

Human analogies

- The triangle/ shamrock/H_2O

- The nature of the universe: space, time and matter

- A book: in mind of author, on shelf in library and in imagination of reader

- A house: architect, purchaser and tenant

All analogies ultimately fall to the ground

Three limits:

♦ Human language is limited

♦ Limits of our own understanding and intellects

♦ Limits of our own finite world and our finite minds

III. IS IT RELEVANT?

Sheds light on the nature of God and his interaction with his creation

♦ The Trinity shows that God is self-sufficient and did not need to create in order to love and communicate

- No single picture or image of God is good enough
- It is the triune God who meets our most fundamental psychological needs as human beings
- It teaches us that there is an inherent threefoldness about every act of God's revelation

CONCLUSION

We can have a full experience of God:

- Experience of the Fatherhood of God (Romans 8:14-16)

- Experience of the love of Christ (Ephesians 3:14-19)

- Experience of the power of the Spirit (Ephesians 3:16; Acts 1:8)

Notes

Notes

Notes

Notes